Creating your UCAS personal statement

Alan Bullock

Trotman Education

£1 Guides: Creating your UCAS personal statement

This first edition published in 2008 by Trotman Education, an imprint of Trotman Publishing, a division of Crimson Publishing Ltd, Westminster House, Kew Road, Richmond, Surrey TW9 2ND

© Trotman Publishing 2008

Reprinted 2009

Author Alan Bullock

British Library Cataloguing in Publication Data
A catalogue record for this book is available from the British Library

ISBN 978-1-906041-42-7

Designed and typeset by Ellipsis Books Ltd, Glasgow
Printed and bound in the UK by Ashford Colour Press, Gosport, Hants

Contents

Contents

Introduction

The key word in personal statement is 'personal'

The aim of this book is to fire you with enthusiasm for presenting yourself in your statement in the best possible way. It will give you ideas about what to write and advice on how to write it, but it won't give you a template or formula. That's because a good personal statement:

- focuses on the specific subject or courses you're applying for and
- is personal to you and has that little stamp of individuality that makes you stand out from everyone else.

As one university put it:

> *There is no such thing as a model statement . . . each one should be different.*

So the book will try to help you make your statement **personal**, to identify your stamp of individuality and to impress it on admissions officers (we'll call them 'selectors' for short) at the universities or colleges to which you are applying. Hopefully the book will make you feel good about what you write, so that you can submit your UCAS application knowing that you've done yourself justice.

If you don't like writing about yourself or think you have nothing special to offer, then the aim is to give you confidence and reassurance, and to help you find your unique selling point or 'USP'. If you **are** confident in your ability to sell yourself, give the book a try anyway. It may give you some extra ideas and you might even discover that what selectors are looking for is not what you thought.

Before we go any further, the most important advice of all is probably **don't leave it to the last minute**. Many applicants will spend weeks developing their statement, not just days and certainly not just a couple of hours.

The purpose of the statement

Focus on the courses you're applying for

The purpose of the statement is to convince the selectors at your chosen universities that you're going to be the kind of student they want to teach.

The difference between a UCAS personal statement and one you might have written in Year 10 or 11 at school is that the focus of the UCAS statement should be more on **why you want to study this course**, not just a summary of your interests and achievements. You probably will write about your outside interests and achievements as part of your statement, but make sure they come across as being relevant to your application in some way, either directly or indirectly.

Many applicants assume that selectors expect personal statements to be written in a very formal style. This is not necessarily true. They want to get a really good feel for the person you are and the way your mind works, so try and write it in a way that comes naturally to you and that **sounds like you**. Don't write things that you wouldn't say in real life, as it won't sound personal.

Also be aware of one selector's warning:

> *If an adult has helped you to write it, we can tell.*

It's very useful to get advice from your teachers, advisers or parents, but don't let them rewrite it for you in their own words because it will sound like them, not you. **Do** check your spelling, punctuation and grammar thoroughly and get someone to proof-read it.

Whatever you do, don't be tempted to cheat by copying from the internet, from someone else's statement or from this or any other book on personal statements. UCAS now uses plagiarism-detection software to scrutinise every application, so you will probably be caught out. You may have heard about the 200 students who applied for Medicine and claimed that their interest in chemistry had begun when they burned a hole in their pyjamas. They had all copied it from the same source. Don't do it.

Some universities are becoming more transparent about what they look for in the personal statement and have published handouts, articles, booklets, web pages or UCAS Entry Profiles giving helpful advice. Do seek out these resources and follow their guidelines and, if you can't find anything that relates to your chosen course or university, look around for others. They may give you some good ideas about how to approach it.

Which leads us nicely on to Chapter 2.

2

Tips from universities

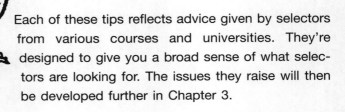

Each of these tips reflects advice given by selectors from various courses and universities. They're designed to give you a broad sense of what selectors are looking for. The issues they raise will then be developed further in Chapter 3.

The personal statement *is* important

Only a minority of courses hold interviews, so most selectors will base their decision purely on your UCAS application. Because of this, the statement is often **the** deciding factor. As one very popular course explained:

> *When you've got 1500 applicants for 75 places, then at the end of the day it's down to the personal statement.*

Some courses that lead to professional qualifications now go one step further by using a strict **marking policy** for assessing your statement against the criteria they're looking for.

Even when it's not considered so important, the statement may become vital at a later stage:

> *We're more interested in your grades and reference than your personal statement. But where the statement becomes crucial is if you don't quite get the grades we ask for, as we will then look at it closely before we decide whether or not to accept you.*

So, whichever way you look at it, it's highly important.

Demonstrate enthusiasm and individuality

The following tips are self-explanatory and build on the advice already given:

> *What we really like is something that makes you stand out.*

> *Most of all, we are looking for people who can demonstrate enthusiasm for the subject.*

> *We're looking for people who have a passion for their subject, who are serious about studying but who also have a life.*

> *A genuine interest in the course is the most important thing, but applicants can express this in many different ways.*

> *Admissions officers are busy, so you need to grab their attention. What is it that makes you different?*

There are no rules for what to put in your statement, but a bit of originality, individuality and personality are so important.

We want to know what makes you tick.

Or, as one mathematics selector put it:

*Tell me **why** you like maths.*

Think carefully about structure and content

Here are some initial tips on how to construct your statement:

Organise your material, structure it, don't waffle, give us an insight into your mind and sound interesting.

Content is more important than style, but we don't object to a bit of style if the content is there.

First impressions count . . . give us a picture of who you are . . . take time and care . . . edit it and don't try to cram everything in.

So:

- structure is important
- be selective and don't waffle
- content is more important than style.

Again Chapter 3 will examine this in more detail.

Tips on specific issues

The next four tips require no further explanation:

> *If you're applying for deferred entry, explain your gap year plans.*

> *If you're dyslexic, don't hide it! Be open and honest. We won't count it against you and we're more likely to be able to provide for your needs.*

> *If you've had relevant work experience, we want to know what you learned from it.*

> *If you're applying for a joint or combined honours programme, talk about both subjects.*

But this one is more controversial:

> *Avoid using quotes.*

What some selectors dislike about quotes is if you do it just for effect or to try and sound clever, for example by opening your statement with a quotation by your favourite writer, historian or economist. But, if used to make a particular point in a reflective way, it might actually be effective. It goes back to the issue of content and style. In other words, don't use a quotation just to try and make you look good. It won't. However, it may be OK to use one if it helps you to explain an important point. The same applies to the use of humour:

> *Don't be quirky – some admissions officers like it but some don't, so it's risky. And don't use lots of exclamation marks.*

This tip seems to be saying that you shouldn't use humour. But in some situations it can work really well. Again, it's not a rule; it's a matter of using careful judgement. This issue will also be picked up again in Chapter 3, but the point about exclamation marks is a good one. Don't use them as a way of trying to sound funny.

> *What you say in your personal statement is very likely to give interviewers an opportunity to form some of their questions.*

If your course is one of the minority that holds interviews, then this is crucial advice. Make sure you keep a copy of your application and be ready to justify and elaborate on everything you say in your statement.

Balance your academic and extra-curricular interests

Consider these tips:

> *We want to get a clear impression of the reasons why you want to study the subject and to see extra-curricular interests or achievements that show you are a well-rounded person.*

Do talk about your personal achievements, because what you gain from wider university life is important.

I like to see a 50/50 split between academic interests and personal interests.

We want at least 70% academic interests and no more than 30% personal interests.

Don't spend more than the last 20% of your statement on those extra-curricular activities and skills which make you a "rounded" person.

So it's clear that selectors are very concerned to see an appropriate balance, but there is disagreement as to what the balance should be, which again proves that there are no rules and that you should use careful judgement. Which should it be . . . 50/50, 70/30, 80/20 or none of these? See Chapter 3.

Show that you know what they want ... and that you've got it

A degree in aerospace engineering will require a different set of interests and qualities from a degree in American studies. So, to provide a focus for your statement, an important starting point is to research and identify the kind of interests and qualities that will be needed by your chosen course and then to:

Tell us why you want to study the subject and demonstrate that you have some of the skills you need to be successful.

How do you know what skills you need to be successful? Here are three suggestions:

- Refer to the **Entry Profile** that many university courses will have on the UCAS website and use your statement to demonstrate how you meet the given criteria. Entry Profiles vary in quality, but some spell out exactly what's required.
- Explore universities' own **websites, prospectuses, course booklets** or other publications, as some of these will also tell you exactly what your chosen course is looking for.
- Go to some **open days** and ask!

Whatever you do, don't give the impression that you have an unrealistic perception about what the course, subject or profession involves. For example, being good at sport is not essential for physiotherapy or even PE teaching. That doesn't mean you should avoid mentioning sporting achievement in your statement but, if you include it, then consider **why** you think it's relevant.

For all subjects, especially very popular ones like law or medicine, the skills, interests, achievements or experiences that you write about in your statement should all provide **evidence** that you've got what they want. The only way you'll know what they want is by researching it. So keep this in mind as we move on to Chapter 3.

ORDER FORM

10% OFF
WHEN YOU ORDER ONLINE!

Win a place on your dream course

Our essential guides help you get into the course and university you dream of

Choosing Your Degree Course & University

This is an ideal resource for any prospective students unsure of what or where they want to study, and is a companion to *Degree Course Offers*. These books enable you to make that first important step of deciding, then securing, a place at the university of your choice.

Author: Brian Heap
ISBN: 978 1 84455 157 6
Pub date: May 2008
Price: £22.99

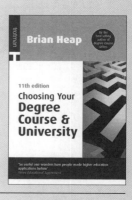

Degree Course Offers 2009 entry

This is the definitive guide to higher education entry. Written by Brian Heap, the guru of higher education, it contains all the information and advice applicants need in order to draw up a shortlist of courses and win a place at the university of their choice.

Author: Brian Heap
ISBN: 978 1 84455 158 3
Pub date: May 2008
Price: £29.99

How to Complete Your UCAS Application 2009 entry

This book gives the inside track on making your UCAS application, providing in-depth advice on navigating the Apply system and avoiding common mistakes. It guides you step by step, from the very early stages of the decision-making process through the ins and outs of completing and submitting your application to results day and beyond.

ISBN: 978 1 84455 160 6
Pub date: June 2008
Price: £12.99

Getting Into Oxford & Cambridge

This unique and bestselling title is a must-read for students wishing to apply to the two most prestigious universities in the country. It covers in detail everything students need to know to win a place including undergraduate colleges and courses and how to decide which to apply for.

Author: Natalie Lancer
ISBN: 978 1 84455 165 1
Pub date: June 2008
Price: £12.99

Students' Money Matters 08/09

This book offers a wide range of financial advice to help students pay their way through university. Key features include information on how much university will cost, borrowing money, taking a year out, thrift tips from current students and advice on budgeting with examples of real student budgets from around the country.

Author: Gwenda Thomas
ISBN: 978 1 84455 166 8
Pub date: June 2008
Price: £16.99

Getting Into the UK's Best Universities & Courses

This book helps students who set their university goals very high by offering course- and institution-specific advice on ways of maximising your chances of success. Packed full of information not available anywhere else, this exciting new book is a must-have for all the most talented, ambitious and dedicated applicants!

Author: Beryl Dixon
ISBN: 978 1 84455 179 8
Pub date: August 2008
Price: £12.99

Ways To Order

 Visit **www.trotman.co.uk** and enter voucher code **CU1W/08** to get 10% off your order (exclusive web offer only)

 Call 0870 900 2665 quoting ISBNs and your credit card details

 Send your completed order form with payment to Trotman Orders, NBN International, Plymbridge House, 10 Estover Road, Plymouth PL6 7PY

ISBN	TITLE	PRICE	QTY	VALUE
978 1 84455 157 6	CHOOSING YOUR DEGREE COURSE & UNIVERSITY	£22.99		
978 1 84455 158 3	DEGREE COURSE OFFERS 2009 ENTRY	£29.99		
978 1 84455 160 6	HOW TO COMPLETE YOUR UCAS APPLICATION 2009 ENTRY	£12.99		
978 1 84455 165 1	GETTING INTO OXFORD & CAMBRIDGE	£12.99		
978 1 84455 166 8	STUDENTS' MONEY MATTERS 08/09	£16.99		
978 1 84455 179 8	GETTING INTO THE UK'S BEST UNIVERSITIES & COURSES	£12.99		

TOTAL

P&P: £3.00 for the first book plus £1.00 per book for each additional book up to a maximum of £10

Delivery: If you are ordering more than one book, please note that your order will only be despatched when all books are published. Please contact us on the number above for the extra postage costs, should you want books sent out when available

P&P

GRAND TOTAL

YOUR DETAILS

Title:

Name:

Delivery address:

Postcode:

Email address:

Phone number:

☐ I would like to receive Trotman's e-newsletter

WAYS TO PAY

REFERENCE CODE: **CU1/08**

By credit card:

Credit Card: ☐ MASTERCARD ☐ AMEX ☐ VISA ☐ SWITCH/MAESTRO
(please underline card type)

Card Number:

Expiry Date:

Switch/Maestro Start Date:

Switch/Maestro Issue no: 3 digit security no:

Card Holder's Name & Address (if different to above):

Signed: Date: /   /

☐ **By cheque:** Please make cheques payable to Trotman Directory

10% DISCOUNT ONLINE AT WWW.TROTMAN.CO.UK

Content

Why should we select you?

You have a maximum of 47 lines or 4,000 characters including spaces. So what do you include? Well, there are three factors that selectors tend to agree on:

- What they want to know is: 'Why do you want to study our course and why should we select you?' So everything in your statement should relate in some way to this, either directly or indirectly.
- Some applicants don't focus enough on their academic interests. For many courses a 50/50 or 60/40 split would be about right, in other words **at least** 50% academic interests and **no more than** 50% personal interests. Some universities actually recommend that a 70/30 or 80/20 split would be best, especially if you are applying for a very competitive academic course. Even 90/10 or 100/0 could be OK if you prefer to devote your statement to explaining why you are passionate about your subject. On the other hand it's good to write about your extra-curricular activities too.

They show that you are a three-dimensional person and they will add impact to your statement, especially if you can link them back to the courses you're applying for.

- Selectors may have to read hundreds of statements, so try to make yours interesting. They want to get an insight into your mind, your personality and what you **think** (not just what you do). Be enthusiastic and try to include things that make you different from everyone else. Everyone is unique, so what's unique about you? What's **your** USP?

Collecting ideas and identifying your USP

You could start by making notes under different headings. If you wish, use **some** of the six headings on the following pages. Remember though, this is not a template for writing your statement, it's just a way of starting to collect ideas. So:

- **You don't have to use all six headings.** For example, if you think your work experience is irrelevant or you haven't got any career plans, then don't write about them.
- **They don't have to be in this order.** Do it your way.
- **If you can devise your own headings, all the better.** You don't want your statement to have the same layout as everyone else who has read this book. If any of your five choices has a booklet, web page or UCAS Entry Profile that tells you what they're looking for, then take your headings from there instead.

Some possible headings are discussed on the next page.

1. Your motives for wanting to study the courses you have chosen

- One way of doing this, but only if it's relevant to you, is to focus on what has inspired you. Was it an event, a lesson, a book, a writer, a place, a visit, an open day, a holiday, a talk, a part-time job, a project, a work experience placement or something else? If so, describe it and also mention anything that has subsequently reinforced or increased your interest. (If it was a film or TV programme, make sure it's not one that hundreds of other applicants are going to write about too.)
- Try to engage with the content of the courses you're applying for. What appeals to you about studying them at degree level? What topics or specialisms interest you and why?
- If you're applying for a subject you already study, describe what you like about it. For example, you could write about particular issues, topics or assignments that have interested you or a field trip or project that you've enjoyed. Or you could focus on specific books, writers, directors or theorists that have made an impact on you. Then, if you can, try to go **beyond** your current syllabus and talk about your own independent reading, personal interest, research or other insights into the subject.

- If you're applying for something you haven't studied before, then it's even more important to talk about your interest and background reading into the subject and to reflect on why you want to study it.
- Otherwise just express your **enthusiasm** for the course or subject you have chosen or express what appeals to you about the prospect of going to university in general.

2. Have you selected your universities for a particular reason?

- If you've chosen five specific universities because their courses are all sandwich courses or modular courses, or they all assess you on coursework not exams, or they're all campus universities, or because of their content, or because you want to stay at home or for some other reason, you could mention this and maybe elaborate on it.

3. Your academic skills and qualities

- Can you demonstrate some skills and qualities that are essential or desirable for your chosen course? If so, write about them in an interesting way or give actual examples as evidence, such as by describing a particular situation when you demonstrated them.
- Can you show how you've learned good **study skills**, either in general or specific to your subject?

- Can you show how you've taken responsibility for your own learning (an essential skill in higher education)?
- Can you identify relevant skills, qualities, knowledge or confidence that **any** of your school or college courses have given you (even if you're not carrying them on as part of your degree)? If so, write about this and explain it.
- Have you ever produced an essay or project that you were quite proud of or made a valuable contribution to a group assignment?
- Did you have a weakness that you've learned to overcome while at school or college?
- Has Learning Support been helpful in overcoming a difficulty you had?
- Have your current subjects combined especially well together?
- If something has disrupted your studies, you could mention this in your statement. Remember to express it in positive terms, such as how you overcame it, and don't give excuses. Better still, ask if it can be explained in your reference instead, so you don't have to put it in your statement at all.

4. Work experience, part-time job or other 'career insights'

- If you've had **relevant** work experience or a **relevant** part-time job, talk about it and **reflect on it**. What skills or qualities have you learned or demonstrated? What have you observed? What have you learned from it? What has impressed you? What has surprised you? How has it changed your perceptions? How has it changed you?

- If you can link it with your recent studies, such as explaining **how** your experience on a cardiac ward reinforced what you learned about the heart in AS biology, all the better.

- If you've had experience or a part-time job that **isn't** directly related to your chosen course, do write about it, but only if you feel it's saying something relevant about your skills and qualities. If it doesn't add anything useful, leave it out.

- Try to avoid bland comments such as 'dealing with customers has improved my communication skills'. Instead be specific by describing a situation you've dealt with, how you cope with pressure, how you manage your time, why you work well in a team or **how** your communication skills have improved . . . or something else that's relevant to your future studies or student life.

- Be aware that Young Enterprise, community work, a conference you attended, a project that involved contact with an employer, a visit to the law courts, a production you took part in, an event you helped to run or an article you wrote and so on, could be just as relevant as 'work experience' and could add real value to your statement, as long as you **reflect on it**.

- Consider whether it's best to give brief details of all your insights, or to focus in more detail on one or two. You could do a combination of both. For example, a drama selector will not be impressed by a list of parts you've played if you don't also convey a sense of what you want to gain from **studying** drama; or a dentistry selector might be more impressed by your observations on what you learned from watching one filling than from a list of all the procedures you saw.

5. Extra-curricular interests

- Do talk about your other interests, experiences, hobbies or achievements. They can demonstrate relevant skills, qualities or knowledge. They can also show that you're someone who will put a lot into (and get a lot out of) your time at university and that you can cope with academic study while also having a life.
- If there's anything you've ever achieved that nobody else you know has achieved, or if you have a talent that you are quite proud of, write about it.
- Don't just say that you like reading. If you do, be specific.
- If your only interest is shopping, clubbing, socialising, listening to music or watching Premiership football, leave it out because you will sound like hundreds of other

applicants, unless you can say it in an interesting and academically relevant way. However, if the team you support is bottom of the North West Counties League and you compile statistics for their website, then that would have real impact as a USP. Even better, add a web link, giving the selector the opportunity to see your work.

- If you still can't think of a USP, then why not take up a new interest? Not only will it improve your personal statement, but it could contribute something to your local community too.

6. Career and/or gap year plans

- Indicate your future career plans if you want to, and if you feel it's relevant, but it's not essential.
- If you're applying for deferred entry (or if you're on a gap year right now), explain why you're taking a gap year or what you are doing/hoping to do in it. Be honest. Don't feel that you have to do something relevant in your gap year, unless you're applying for a course that demands it. It could also be useful to indicate how you intend to keep your reading or study skills active during your gap year.

Now prioritise your material

Don't try to cram everything in. **Be selective**. Choose the points that you feel are most relevant or have the most impact.

Before you decide whether to include something, apply the **'so what?'** factor. For example: 'In my spare time I play badminton.' So what? Does it add something that's relevant to your application? If not, leave it out.

If your first draft is too long, then go through it in great detail and remove every single word that isn't totally necessary.

Some general tips on how to write it . . .

. . . but don't copy any of the examples

Open with an interesting sentence that doesn't begin with 'I' . . .

. . . and doesn't include 'from a young age'.

Explaining how the use of sustainable materials in the new Welsh Assembly building first drew your attention to the relationship between design and the environment would be a more interesting opening than: 'I have wanted to be an architect from a young age.'

Be creative but don't try to be clever

Humour can be very effective, but take care. There's a narrow dividing line between humour that works and humour that doesn't and what makes one selector laugh may irritate another. If you keep putting exclamation marks at the end of sentences, you're being too flippant. Remember the advice in Chapter 2 about quotes or saying something that you couldn't justify if they call you for an interview.

Don't just *say* what you do, *reflect* on what you do

If you're applying for marketing, criminology or anthropology and want to mention your Saturday job in a clothes shop, then try to link your observations in an interesting way. For example, have you noticed how sales promotions influence customers or how different management styles impact on staff motivation? Have you ever caught a shoplifter or observed something interesting about their behaviour? Have you learned some techniques for dealing with awkward customers or persuading people to buy?

Don't state the obvious

When reflecting on what you gained from your work experience in an accounts firm, don't then waste space by saying '… which is a useful skill for a degree in Accountancy'. They know it is. You don't have to spell it out.

Ideally use paragraphs or headings

Paragraphs or headings make it easier to read and it will look more structured, especially if you leave a line in between. But this will also take up more space, so you need to judge it for yourself. It's good to make full use of your 47 lines, but you don't have to. Most importantly, don't waffle or repeat yourself.

Hide your thesaurus

You won't impress selectors with posh vocabulary that you wouldn't use in real life. If you wouldn't use it in normal conversation or discussion, don't put it in your statement as it will make you sound pompous or pretentious.

What about the ending?

One successful Cambridge applicant said that your statement should be like a necklace, where the ending links back to your opening. This is a useful tip. On the other hand many students waste four or five lines by ending with a paragraph that summarises what they've said already or with a rather cheesy declaration about how their time at university is going to fuel them with desire and self-fulfilment. If you really mean it, that's great, but if it's just said for effect, then don't do it. The worst thing to say is: 'As I've already said ...' If you've already said it, don't say it again.

What if you're applying for a mixture of courses?

It's easier to write your statement if you've applied for the same course or subject at all five choices; but, if you're applying for a mixture of courses, put yourself in the position of each selector who will read it.

The best approach is probably to make all of your statement relevant in some way to all of your choices. So instead of writing one paragraph on each choice, keep it more general and talk about issues that are at least indirectly relevant to each choice. If you can't manage this, then seek advice about whether your choices are wise.

If you're applying to four medical, dental or veterinary schools and one other choice, focus your statement entirely on the four. Then check whether the 'fifth choice' will consider you, even though your statement is focused on the others. If they won't, then choose another.

Case studies

Add your own ingredients

To briefly illustrate some of the points that have been made, let's finish with five random examples of students who were offered places by all of their choices:

Laura applied for psychology and works part-time on the fish-counter at Waitrose. Totally irrelevant, you might think, but using the 'So what?' factor, she compared the satisfaction she gets from knowing how to gut and fillet a mackerel with the satisfaction of carrying out statistical analysis of experimental results in A level psychology. This demonstrated individuality, commitment, versatility, numeracy, originality of thought, a desire to learn and an understanding of the skills needed by an undergraduate psychology student. It also added a touch of humour in a serious and relevant way and provided a highly memorable USP.

Mark applied for primary teaching. His first draft lacked impact and only included a short paragraph about his work experience. He then rewrote it, opening with: *'Today I took my first PE lesson with a class of lively Year 5s'* and devoted the next 29 lines to a series of interesting reflections on his experience in a school and a play-scheme.

Kim applied for music and took the risk of opening her statement with *'Hi, I'm Kim and I'm a tuba player.'* She was successful because the rest of her statement was brilliant and also because female tuba players are quite rare, so her USP was established in the opening line. Saying 'Hi' at the start of your statement is definitely not recommended but the **content** of Kim's statement was so good that it minimised the risk.

Dave applied for business management and took great care over his statement. He needed 300 UCAS points to get into his preferred university but only achieved 260. However, he was still given a place and said afterwards: *'My personal statement was the key to being accepted.'*

Lorin applied for law. She only used nine lines to explain her interest in the subject, but she placed it into the context of how she arrived in Britain and the personal challenges she has overcome. It was a unique statement and, although on the surface much of it was not directly about law, the qualities, skills and resilience that it demonstrated were all highly relevant and also made compelling reading. Lorin's advice is: *'Tell your story and add your own ingredients and your personal touch.'*

Finally

Choose the right time to write it

If reading this has made you feel good about writing your statement, then grab the moment and start drafting it. It's always best to work on it when you're feeling positive, but don't write it before you've decided what you're applying for, as the statement should reflect your reasons for choosing the course.

You may have noticed that the book hasn't included a single example of what a statement should look like. That's because, as Lorin said, you now need to select your own ingredients and add your personal touch or, as one university put it: *'Reveal something about yourself.'*

You're unique. Everyone is. So demonstrate this in your statement.

6 Acknowledgements

I wish to thank all the university admissions officers who have shared their perceptions and advice. Equally I want to thank Laura, Mark, Kim, Dave, Lorin, Marianne, Andy, Gurpreet and all the other students who have inspired me, and Carolyn for her patience and support.

AB